# *Dandelions*
## *and* Thistles

Biblical meditations from the Iona Community

*Edited by Jan Sutch Pickard*

Wild Goose Publications

First published by Wild Goose Publications, 1999

ISBN 1 901557 14 6

Cover and illustrations: silk paintings © Mari Girling

**Wild Goose Publications**
Unit 15, Six Harmony Row, Glasgow  G51 3BA

Wild Goose Publications is the publishing division of
**The Iona Community**
Scottish Charity No. SC003794.
Limited Company Reg. No SCO96243.

Distributed in Australia and New Zealand by Willow Connection Pty Ltd, Unit 7A, 3-9 Kenneth Road, Manly Vale NSW 2093.

Permission to reproduce any part of this work in Australia or New Zealand should be sought from Willow Connection.

A catalogue record for this book is available from the British Library.

Printed by The Cromwell Press Ltd, Trowbridge, Wilts.

# Dandelions *and* Thistles

# Contents

# Introduction

Jan Sutch Pickard

How is the Word of God like a dandelion or a thistle? It is pure gold, or royal purple, grows anywhere, cheers the heart when the season is still cold, and spreads like wildfire, with seeds that travel on the winds of the Spirit ...

Wait a minute – aren't dandelions and thistles weeds?

But what is a weed but a flower where you least expect it?

The Trustees of the Abbey grounds on Iona, who keep the lawns so green and well mown in that much-visited place, would probably frown on thistles and dandelions. On the other hand these flowers are carved into the cloisters, to the glory of God and as a sign of God's creation. They flourish in odd corners of Hebridean crofts, and on wasteland in Govan and the other inner-city areas where Iona Community members are committed to work. They may be prickly and inconvenient, and no one would grow them as a cash crop, but they are also cheerful, subversive, resilient. These flowers are signs of the way God works.

But they are not flowers at all.

Or rather, they are members of the family *compositae*, along with daisies and sunflowers; each 'flower' is in fact composed of whole communities of flowers, clustered together, interdependent.

In that way these bright fragments of creation are also like God's Word in the Bible. For the Bible is not a single flower, but a whole bunch; not one word but many; not a simple message, but a whole cluster of different kinds of communication: history, story-telling, letters, prayers. It is poetry and prose, inspired prophecy and down-to-earth proverbs. There are amazing lists – genealogies, or the materials needed to build the temple, or the things

the queen of Sheba had in her luggage.

And somewhere amid all those human words, told over centuries, written down long ago, translated and retranslated, learned by heart and expounded by preachers good, bad and indifferent – somewhere in all that is God's Word, by which we may be inspired to live in God's way.

If the Spirit blows one of these winged seeds our way.

This is why we have compiled this book of biblical meditations. We invited a number of very different people, Members and Associates of the Iona Community, to share ways that the Bible has spoken to them, inspiring them to write original material that can be used in worship. What has emerged is a cluster of very different responses, but all relevant and ready to be used.

The work of the Wild Goose Resource Group is well known and valued, and here you will find new pieces by John Bell: monologues which pick up and reflect on gospel stories. A different voice is heard in Norman Shanks' Zacchaeus, or John Davies' Elijah, or in Ruth Burgess speaking as Mrs Manoah.

There are more complex scenarios, like the editorial meeting about Jonah, which could be presented as plays within the framework of a service. The contributions by both Kathy Galloway and David Osborne could be used in a family service during Advent, with a sequence of reflections giving a different perspective on short Bible readings from the nativity stories, and familiar carols. Similarly the piece called *Follow me*, with linked readings, could form the basis of a service about vocation, and could be interspersed with verses of the Wild Goose song 'Will you come and follow me?'.

The piece based on John 10:7–18, called *We are the*

*Introduction*

*sheep,* was originally written for all-age worship, and was accompanied by enthusiastic miming which took over the whole church building and involved most of the congregation. Why not try this?

Ruth Burgess reflects on the way we see angels. How could this be interpreted visually in worship? Joy Mead has written a sequence of poems about women in the Bible. Those included here could be interpreted with dance, or interspersed with music. Kate MacIlhagga has written prayers which are steeped in biblical language and images – and she suggests symbolic actions to accompany them.

We looked for material that was different, challenging. Apart from the botanical name *compositae,* you will not find here the kind of scholarship that overawes and obscures. You will not find massed bedding-plants of 'churchy' language and well-loved hymns. You will not find smooth green lawns of liturgy. But you will find dandelions and thistles, unofficial flowers, which travel light on the winds of the Spirit and spring up in the most unlikely places.

These meditations sprang up in the imagination of fellow Christians, bloomed in worship on Iona or in Glasgow, in village church or inner-city congregation, at Greenbelt or Glastonbury. And now this book is full of winged seeds, which may touch your heart, take root in your worship, flower to the glory of God, bear fruit, send out more seeds ...

This is how the Word of God spreads.

*Introduction*

9

# The cheerful unrepentant weeds

Jan Sutch Pickard

In the beginning
God saw the cheerful unrepentant weeds:
thistles and dandelions –
and God saw that they were good.
They were fruitful and multiplied.
They bloomed on poor soil
and in the barren wilderness;
they brought colour into a solemn world.

God considers them as well as the lilies –
they don't toil or spin either,
but they breed like rabbits
and spread like wildfire.
Never anxious about tomorrow,
today they reclaim the wasteland,
break through concrete, transform bomb-sites.
They are a treasure hidden in a field.
Common as muck, but clothed in purple and gold,
they proclaim the presence of their creator.

God, open-handed sower of grace,
sees that thistles, flourishing on the field's edge,
won't give stray seeds a chance;
aware of the sparrow's fall,
knows too how the smallest seed of all
grows till it can shelter the birds of the air.
God watches the thistledown,
travelling light, cast adrift on the currents of the air,
finding somewhere to make a fresh start.
God values the dandelions as a harvest:
we cannot live by bread alone,
our souls hunger for beauty and meaning –
we are nourished by signs of the Kingdom.

God, knowing the secret of life and death,
created green shoots that spring up after rain,

*GENESIS 1:11–13, MATTHEW 6:28–30*
*MATTHEW 13:3B–9, 31–32,44; JOHN 12:24*

flowers that follow the sun,
fruits that trust the winds of heaven,
and seeds that will only grow
if they fall in the earth and die.

These weeds – as down-to-earth as you or me –
are parables of the wisdom and work of God.

*The cheerful
unrepentant weeds*

Finally, allow people time to come back to the present and in their own time to return their stones
– into water as an affirmation of baptism;
– or to the foot of (or to form) a cross as a sign of recommitment.

Allow people, if they wish, to say why they chose a particular stone. This may lead to a sharing of the 'journey', if it feels safe – but don't push it.

Remember the
Rock from which
you were hewn

# Elijah's story

John Davies

*1 Kings 18, 19*

Things had been going incredibly well for me. I had won a landslide victory over the opposition. They had co-ordinated all their resources; all their leaders, political and religious, had ganged up against me. They represented all that was false. Their Baalism stood for the concentration of power in the hands of a few wealthy magnates, while the peasants who did the real work had no voice, no vote and no land. Their religion sanctified cruelty and injustice. I was called to put all my energy into destroying it. And I won. I killed all their prophets, all four hundred and fifty of them. Four hundred and fifty – against one. And I won.

Then I climbed to the top of Mount Carmel, to be able to make an accurate weather forecast. I came down the mountain as the rain started to break the long drought. The king, Ahab, had his fast chariot and tried to get back home to the capital city before he got wet through. But I found that I could run as fast as any chariot, and I got there before him.

What a triumph! What a victory! What a confirmation that I had been right all the time, when I seemed to be entirely alone in the face of national falsehood and depravity.

And then I heard that one woman had set her heart on destroying me. One woman, against me, who had beaten all those men. But it knocked all the energy and confidence out of me. I was limp and helpless. I had to flee for my life. I ran from the city, from the meeting places, from the cultivated land. I came to the edge of the desert. And I went on, another twenty miles or more. In the sun-baked desert, I found a little bush; if I sat under it, there was enough shade to protect me. This was the end, I thought. My success had faded away. It counted for nothing. I realised that, in spite of a moment's triumph, against the forces of evil you can never win. I was a failure, like everyone before me. They had not been able to stand up against all that was wrong in the world, and I had done no better. So I made my prayer: 'It is enough: now, Lord, take my life, for I am no better than my ancestors before me.'

That prayer settled me: I was able to sleep.

The next thing I knew was this angel waking me up and telling me to get up for breakfast. Breakfast? Where was that going to come from – in the desert? But, sure enough, somehow there was some sort of bread roll, and a jar of water, all ready for me. So I nibbled at the bread and took a few sips of the water. There was nothing else to do, so I went back to sleep. Not for long: the angel was back again, telling me off for not finishing my breakfast. 'You've got to have a good breakfast if you're going to do a good day's work' ... but I was not planning on any work – all I wanted to do was die. However, the angel made it clear that I was not going to have a nice quiet death. I was to be on the road again. That was what the breakfast was for. And it was a long road. I was on that road forty days and forty nights. I landed up at Mount Horeb, God's home in the desert.

I found a cave in that hillside. I was able to crawl into it and curl up. It was like going back into the womb. I could feel secure, curled up on myself. I felt happy and safe with my messed-up sick self. I was alone with the wounds which were the only possessions left to me. This would be a nice way to die.

Suddenly the question in my ear: it must be from God: 'WHAT ARE YOU DOING HERE?'

Put like that, it sounds like being interrogated by

*Elijah's story*

19

the police. But I didn't feel it that way. It was a sensible, enquiring question, which needed a straightforward answer. So I told my story:

'I'm here because I've been so keen to stand up for the true God. All your people have abandoned you; they have ruined your places of worship; they have killed all your ministers; I am the only one left, and they are chasing me, to kill me too.'

There was only one thing still true about me, that I was alone and hated; all my securities and successes had failed. There was no moral basis left for me. The only thing left was my death-wish.

The voice came back: 'Get out of that hole, and stand up straight on the mountain, and face God.'

I knew that God was very close. And it was chaos. It was terrifying. There was a powerful wind: it broke up the landscape. All the things around me, on the horizontal plane, were smashed: they lost their solidity: there was nothing left for me to hold on to. But I realised that God was not in the wind. It happened, but God was outside it. And then there was an earthquake. All the earth's structure was smashed: everything vertically below me lost its solidity; there was nothing left on which I could firmly place my feet. But I realised that God was not in the earthquake. It happened, but God was outside it. And then there was fire: the very basic nature of things was smashed: the reliable liquids and solids were turned into insubstantial gas. The very elements that I myself was made of were shown to be fragile, vulnerable, flimsy. But I realised that God was not in the fire. It happened, but God was outside it.

After all this, there was nothing left but a gentle

*Elijah's story*

20

murmuring sound. And that was God. God was the alternative to all that chaos.

So I did uncurl myself, and I went out and stood up straight at the cave's entrance. I picked up my cloak and wrapped it round my face: the dust had not settled - I was almost choking.

And the same patient questioning came at me: 'WHAT ARE YOU DOING HERE?'

The wind and earthquake and fire had not changed the question. So they did not change my answer:

'I'm here because I have been so keen to stand up for the true God. All your people have abandoned you; they have ruined your places of worship; they have killed all your ministers; I am the only one left, and they are chasing me to kill me too.'

But this time, there was something more. There was a job for me to do. I was told to go back into the political arena, and take responsibility for a change of government. There were specific people who had to be found and put into positions of leadership. There was a plan, and a future. I was no longer alone. I was told that there were seven thousand colleagues and allies on whom I could count.

What made all the difference to me was the persistent quiet questioner. The question and the questioner were there after the events of chaos just as before. In one sense, nothing had changed. But my all-embracing depression was lifted: my damaged nature was no longer the main thing that was true about me. I could get on with the job of standing up for a truth and a purpose outside myself. The chaos was not the end of everything,

*Elijah's story*

but the beginning of a new stage of work.

So I went and found Elisha. And that was the start of another story.

*Here are two quite different ways of using this story:*

*– For a **house-group**, all the members of the group prepare by reading 1 Kings 18–19, if possible in a variety of translations, beforehand. Meanwhile one member prepares to tell this version, becoming very familiar with the text and delivering it as a testimony, rather than simply reading it aloud. After a silence, the group discusses new insights into the story.*

*– In **alternative worship**, the story could be told in semi-darkness – the voice of the narrator being more important than his face. Lights and music could be used to emphasise the plot – triumph, fear, chaos, new hope – but never to drown out the words.*

Elijah's story

# Four women

## Joy Mead

*The following four poems, although written originally for private reflection, could form part of a service focusing on women in the Bible, or on the way God calls and uses the most unlikely people. The first poem could be linked to prayers of confession, the second and third to praise and thanksgiving, the fourth to prayers of intercession. They could also be accompanied by instrumental music, or interpreted by dance.*

*Following the four Old Testament passages, which would in each case need to precede the poems, the Magnificat (Luke) could be read, and the congregation could sing 'Tell out my soul the greatness of the Lord' (Timothy Dudley Smith). Other appropriate hymns to intersperse with the readings might be 'Guide me O thou great Jehovah' (William Williams) or 'Out of the depths I cry to thee' (Martin Luther) or 'Deep in the shadows of the past' (Brian Wren) or the song 'Stand O stand firm' (Wild Goose Resource Group: Many and Great).*

*To lighten the mood the service could include 'God it was who said to Abraham' (Wild Goose Resource Group: Love from Below). But these poems are most appropriate for a quiet and reflective act of worship.*

# Songlines for Sarah and Hagar

Joy Mead

GENESIS 18:11–14 AND 21:1–20A

From the immense shadows
the sound of a desperate cry
cuts across Sarah's laughter
and the dance on the green.

The sorrowing one shapes suffering's sound
to the song of the earth
and the way of the people's dreams
while the lost one searches still,
for priests and altars
and words
that will not betray.

But the priests are all unfrocked
and the altars somewhere else
and only the earth's echoing wail
sings the way back
along untrodden paths
to inspiration and recovery
of lost knowledges.
For hope is not mine to bring
but to recognise in the sharing
of bread with Hagar
who suffers, and hopes, and waits
at the margins.

*The two Old Testament stories on which this is
based form a powerful contrast. The glimpses they
give into human hope and suffering deserve a
thoughtful silence, not many words of explanation.
Music by a solo instrument might be a good
accompaniment for a reading of the two Bible
passages followed by the poem.*

# Pharaoh's daughter

Joy Mead

They are everywhere;
small Hebrew children,
lifeblood of a people,
fertile, fecund, flowing:
a river of life
she walks beside.

The basket: a floating flower,
comes towards her on the stream,
offering its contents
like a promise.

Her hands reach out
disturbing the glistening flow.
Broody birds rise,
their wings beating wildly
like her startled heart
as she draws the baby
from the water

Then the girl, her eyes alert
from minding, moves
to her side, whispering
of mother's milk

While she, childless
daughter of Pharaoh,
longs to feed honey
to another woman's child.

The wind off the water
caresses her urgency
with the coolness
of time that is always early
and will neither allow her to pass by
nor let her claim this abundance

*EXODUS 2:1–10*

as if it were her own.

She gives him back
to the stream of life;
to be nourished
in the knowledge and resilience
he will need, to survive
and lead his people
to freedom.

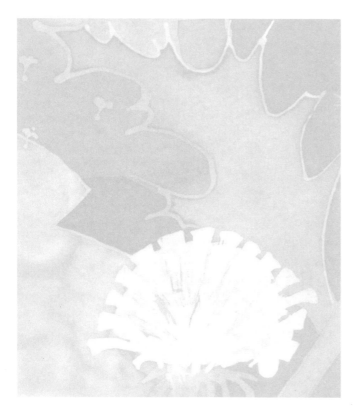

*Pharaoh's daughter*

# Miriam's song

Joy Mead

Miriam singing; Miriam dancing;
Miriam wonderer
walking on air.

Miriam laughing; Miriam crying;
Miriam wanderer
walking on earth.

Miriam watching; Miriam minding;
Miriam prophetess:
crafting her story.

Stepping out lightly,
pulsing with beauty,
wise and far seeing,
going before us;

Trusting the dance,
willing and dreaming,
filling all lands
with the music of hope.

*This poem on its own would work well in a service
where dance is also used – not to accompany the
dance, but maybe as a bridge between the words of
the Old Testament and movement and music.*

*Exodus 15:1–2; 11–13; 19–21*

# Sisera's mother

Joy Mead

Who does not cast a glance
to where an unnamed mother sits
silently at the edge of her story.

Pondering in her heart
the things of his growing, she waits,
powerless and voiceless,
for the hoofbeat of his horses
on the soil of home;
while talk is of damsels
and dyed stuff
to grace a victor's neck;

She watches the dawning:
the gradual revealing
of a vast emptiness,
for many share the dying
but few the knowing.

The rays of the morning sun
pierce her heart
and her still body is the shape
of a multitude of grieving women;
for no one asks the mothers when the talk is of war.

JUDGES 5:19–22; 24–31

28

# Mrs Manoah's story

Ruth Burgess

My name – it's not recorded. My husband's is though – he's called Manoah. He comes from Zorah and we lived in Israel. It was a bad time politically – the Philistines ruled Israel and gave us little peace.

We'd been married a long time – enjoyed each other's company. Sadly we'd had no children. But we kept trying ...

Anyway, the day I'm remembering had been a peculiar day. I'd been badly frightened. A stranger had come to our house. Manoah was out in the fields and I was alone. He scared me, this man. He said he had a message for me – that I would soon be pregnant and that I'd have a son. Then he said that while I was pregnant I had to watch what I ate and drank. I was about to tell him that I knew all about eating for two and odd food-cravings and the rest – after all I'd been trying long enough to get pregnant and I knew all about it in theory – when he came out with this amazing list. I was to drink no wine, no beer, and as for food, no pork, no vulture meat, no camels, no seagulls, no cormorants, no badgers ... I began to think he was crazy. Who in their right mind would ever fancy a seagull sandwich? And then he went on about how this boy was to be brought up. It was to be according to the teaching of some fundamentalist sect. He was not to touch corpses or ever have a haircut. I tell you, it was weird.

He told me nothing about himself, this stranger: not where he'd come from, who sent him – nothing. He just talked to me, told me all these things and he left. I tell you, he put the shivers up and down my spine – that's a fact.

I decided that I'd better tell Manoah about this stranger and what he'd said ... so I did. I'd begun to wonder if all this had something to do with God. I remembered an ancestor of mine who'd also had a

*Mrs Manoah's story*

visit from some strangers, with a similar message. She'd just laughed. But she'd had a child sure enough – Isaac, I think he was called.

When I'd finished telling the story to Manoah, I think he must have had similar thoughts to me. So he decided to ask God what it was all about. He began to pray – something neither of us had done for a long time.

'God,' he said, 'God, if you sent this stranger to my wife, will you send him back again please, and this time I want to meet him too.' Not quite the prayer I'd have prayed – but at least I'd have company if the stranger returned.

Well, God must have heard him, for sure enough the stranger did come back. I was in the fields this time – on my own again – but not for long. I ran and found Manoah very quickly and he came back with me and started asking the stranger who he was: 'Are you the man who was talking to my wife?' he said. I grinned – perhaps Manoah was a bit jealous! But it felt good. When the man said yes, Manoah asked him about the things he'd told me.

'If your words come true,' he said to the man, 'how do we bring our child up?' Manoah got the whole story: no beer, no wine, no haircut, no rabbits, no starfish, no bats, no ostriches, no corpses, no butterflies ... the list was even stranger than before.

And still the man would not say who he was. In the end Manoah asked him to stay for lunch. He suggested roast goat – at least that wasn't on the banned list – but the stranger said no and suggested that we burn the goat as an offering to God ...

Manoah tried to question him again: 'Who are you? Tell us your name and then we'll know who to thank if your words come true.' But the stranger was still evasive. He said that his name was a name of mystery, a name of wonder – well, he was certainly mysterious and we were definitely wondering!

Manoah went and found a goat and killed it – put it on a rock with some grain and lit the fire under it. And then the stranger made his move ... he walked straight into the flame and disappeared – frightened the life out of us; just disappeared in the flames and smoke. And we never saw him again.

Manoah panicked. He thought we'd had it: 'We've seen an angel – we've seen God,' he said. 'We're sure to die.'

But we didn't die – it would have been a bit daft if we had. After all why would God bother to show us and tell us what he did – and then kill us? No sense, my Manoah sometimes, no sense.

And you know it happened. We had our son – Sammy we called him – and he grew up straight and strong. He had his moments – a bit of a long-haired layabout sometimes, a bit of a daredevil, quite a womaniser and no respect for ancient buildings, our Sammy.

But that ... that's another story.

*The congregation will share the puzzlement and surprise of Mr and Mrs Manoah if this story is told without any biblical reference being given. At the end they can be asked whether they think they know 'Sammy', by what name, and what else they know about him. The context of this story might be the retelling of the rest of the Samson legend, but it could be a service celebrating the way that God involves ordinary people in the story of salvation. A Wild Goose song which could be used is 'The strangest of saints' (Wild Goose: Heaven Shall Not Wait).*

*Mrs Manoah's story*

# Jonah

John Davies

*A meeting of the Editorial Board, to decide whether a draft text entitled 'The Book of Jonah' is acceptable for inclusion within the canon of Holy Scripture. The board consists of Isaiah, Jeremiah, Nahum and Zephaniah.*

**Nahum**   I took this text back home last night and read it to my wife. We were both shocked and disgusted. I've never come across such filthy, unpatriotic stuff. It gives the impression that God actually sympathises with the Ninevites. What have our lads been fighting for all these years? Nineveh's a bloodstained slut, and God will pelt it with filth. Tear this stuff up. It's dangerous rubbish.

**Zephaniah**   You're lucky. My wife – silly cow – read this thing and thought it was taking the mickey out of the clergy. She laughed like a drain. She went to sleep chuckling over it. That shows it can't possibly do as Holy Scripture. But don't let's waste too much time on such drivel. We know that Nineveh is finished. Once a Ninevite always a Ninevite – they won't change, and it's plain stupid to suggest they ever can.

**Jeremiah**   Sorry, but before we write it off, I must point out one thing. We aren't God. God is like a potter, and he can change the character of people if he wants to. People can change; that part of the book seemed to me to be worth saying.

**Isaiah**   I would put it more strongly myself. Do you think God wants this whole part of the world to be a permanent wasteland? There's no future for us unless the big powers around us stop tearing each other apart. As I see it, the time must come when there will be the three of us at peace: we, little

Israel, will be on a level with Assyria and Egypt; and when that happens, it will be a blessing for the whole world.

**Zephaniah**   All right, suppose, just *suppose,* that that could happen; it still doesn't get us very far on the present item on our agenda, which is this stupid book of Jonah. We seem to be split, two against two – and none of us has a casting vote. We shall have to broaden our consultation.

**Jeremiah**   Perhaps we had better start with Jonah himself in that case. He's a professional prophet. He should have some opinion about the picture of himself that's given in this story.

**Jonah**   I protest! I've never been so insulted in all my life. Here I was, a nice, quiet domestic prophet for King Jeroboam. And now this story is going to be splashed all over the place, accusing me of disobedience to God, discourtesy to a foreign power, inhumane attitudes to plants and animals, and I don't know what else. If this goes into print, I'll sue.

**Jeremiah**   Come off it. You can't do too badly, compared to some of us. You're not a coward; you go straight off on a risky sea-voyage; you pay the full fare ...

**Nahum**   ... and your heart's in the right place (unlike some I could mention). You do want our enemies to be ground into the dust; you do want bad people to stay bad, so that they can get what's coming to them. If the opposition is going to repent all the time, what's going to happen to our political system?

*Jonah*

**Sailors**   Here, can we get a word in edgeways? Mister Jonah, squire, we're in solidarity with you, mate. You treated us fair. We don't always get along with the fare-paying elements, but you were a true one. As for the rest of you holy growlers, we may be dirty pagans in your precious eyes, but sometimes we can see quality better than you can.

**David**   Just in passing, gentlemen, can I put in a good word for the nice psalm which your author has managed to fit in? I always thought I'd written 151 – or was it 152? – and now we have this missing one saved for posterity. Good show.

**Ninevites**   We know that some of you think we should be lying six feet deep, but we do have an angle ourselves, you know. We get a bad press, because most of us are ignorant, and we have more than our fair share of sleaze. But when the crunch comes, we can turn round double quick. What's more, we are a democratic tribe. We don't wait for the King to tell us what to do – no, when we move, the King moves. We common people have more influence on government than some of you would credit. You may think you have got God's spirit. We're telling you, you're not the only ones. We know what it's like to be shifted by God's spirit – and we take our government along with us too.

*General commotion. Invasion of boardroom by miscellaneous collection of fish, worms, gourds, sun, etc.*

**Fish, etc.**   We protest. We object. We call for a ban. This author treats us as if we are just at the beck and call of irresponsible clots like this Jonah.

*Jonah*

We are honourable creatures. We don't exist just to satisfy the fancies of storytellers. We are fed up with this kind of autocratic manipulation by humans. Watch out. We'll get you.

**Isaiah**  Dear creatures, yes, we do see your point of view. You have every right to be what God has made you. But you are so much more intelligent than typical humans such as Jonah, so perhaps you can forgive God for using you sometimes to teach humans a lesson.

**Nahum**  Now you're bringing God into it. Isn't it about time we called him in to get his point of view? After all, he is a main character, and I expect he is pretty fed up with the kind of picture of himself that is given in this story. I say that this story brings God into disrepute.

**The Lord**  Thank you; that is very courteous of you. May I say that, while I appreciate your concern, I really am quite happy about featuring in this story. I see it as a joke, and I do like to hear the angels laughing. Also, I'm not sorry that you have such divided opinions about it. A good story will always put the responsibility on you, and the way you react to it tells me a lot about you. When my Son comes, he will tell you plenty of stories to make you think. I hope he will make you laugh, too. Above all, people like you, Nahum and Zephaniah, do have to realise that I am the God of the Second Chance, and I really do want people like the Ninevites to have the opportunity to change their ways – and to change their government into the bargain. I'm sorry for Jonah; but at least he shows that I can use grudging and unpleasant people just as much as I can use all

*Jonah*

you nice and proper characters. Do give my love to your wife, Zephaniah; she sounds like a girl after my own heart.

**The Author**   I think it's only fair that I should get a word in, though after that last contribution there's not much that I can add. I'm grateful for all the comments, but I am not proposing any amendments to the text. But let me say this to you, Nahum and Zephaniah: I know that you are going to have your books included. I'm not against that, although I'm sorry you feel you have to take the line you do. All I ask for is that my angle should be included as well. Let people make of it what they will.

**Jeremiah**   So it looks as if we shall go on having to have things in the Scriptures which look at first sight as if they cancel each other out. I suppose we are getting used to this – it's all over the place, in Genesis and Samuel and so on. It's going to look untidy. I only hope that when people later on come and pick up the Scriptures they will see the point. I hope they keep their churches thoroughly untidy as well.

**Nahum**   Very good. Are we all agreed? Next item on the agenda?

*This could be performed in worship as it stands. But it is based on experience in Bible study and could be handled as follows:*

*Read the whole Book of Jonah, in parts, as printed in the Dramatised Bible. Then form teams, of two or more people each, to represent at least the main characters (Nahum, Zephaniah, Jeremiah,*

*Jonah*

*Isaiah, Jonah, Sailors, Ninevites, the Lord and the Author) and, if possible, David, the Fish, the Worm, the Gourd, the Sun. Each team can take its script in the dialogue as the starting-point for getting into its character. The first four should meet together as the Editorial Board. After a few minutes of getting into its own character, each team should feel at liberty to go round to other teams to form alliances, to express objections, to consult together. All the other teams should visit the Author team and the Editorial Board, to express their opinion on the original question, 'Should this book be included in Holy Scripture?'*

*There could then be a discussion about attitudes in our society, and our churches, which are similar. Do you find the idea of the God of the Second Chance helpful?*

Jonah

# The cup

Yvonne Morland

We come, original clay to Your hand,
ready to be moulded to Your purpose,
wet with the living waters.

Humble, we submit to the power of Your will,
we begin to spin into life.

Awry and out of balance,
we long for your centring touch
yet resist on first contact.

Full of the words and images of the world,
we swing this way and that
till Your firm hand grasps us, pulls us back,
draws us to the centre,
spinning into rings.

Yielding, we spin, begin to sing,
picking up the rhythm,
rising and falling
becoming smooth
forming and filling.

Slowing, we spin,
vessel we become,
vessel to be shared,
full of the living waters.

*Isaiah 64:8*

## Mary and Joseph go to Bethlehem

*READ: LUKE 2:1–5*

*A woman villager from Nazareth speaks*

It wasn't too bad for us. My Reuben just came from Cana. So we thought that leaving early we could get there and back in a day. Well, we didn't. There was no problem getting there, but it was chaos in the village with great queues and a lot of waiting and everyone getting annoyed. Until someone opened a skin of wine.

We finally get to the front and there's a Greek clerk. What does he know? Can't tell a Phoenician from a Pharisee! Try explaining to a Greek clerk that your mother's first husband was your father's brother, but by his father's second wife. Hopeless!

We ended up staying the night. But it was a chance to catch up with those relatives that we usually only see at weddings and funerals. But for some people it was awful. That Joseph bar Jacob came from Judea, and he had to go back. Bethlehem I think it was. And with his wife who was expecting. Ended up having the baby there. That baby must have been early. They hadn't been married eight months! I remember the wedding. It was very sudden for some reason.

Anyway, off they went to Bethlehem. And we didn't see them again for years. I often wondered what happened to them while they were away.

# *Christmas characters*

David Osborne

## No room at the inn

*READ: LUKE 2:6–7*

*A male guest at Bethlehem speaks*

I cannot imagine how anyone could come up with the idea that people should return to their ancestral home for a census. It was no doubt simply an administrative convenience.

The roads were packed with people moving in all directions. And all sorts of people: tradespeople, labourers, farmers – one had to mix with them all.

I sent my man on ahead when I realised there was no getting out of this. He was able to book me a room. Well, they called it a room. It was little more than a cupboard really, with a tiny window, and a strong smell.

Then, would you believe, just as it was getting dark, I was asked if I could move. Could I possibly move out to make way for a pregnant woman? A Galilean, no less! Well, you don't need to hear what I said. But as you can imagine, I did not move out. If these people worked and got some money together; if they planned their lives instead of just reacting to the demands of the moment, they wouldn't end up with nowhere to stay. And of course if you keep helping them they'll never learn.

*Christmas characters*

## Angels come to shepherds

*READ: LUKE 2:8–14*
*A shepherd's wife speaks*

My Jacob never said much about it. He was
often out nights. That's what happens if you're a
shepherd. That's the life: nights, days and poor
pay. And you miss a lot of what goes on in the
village. We heard about what happened, of
course: the angels and the baby and all that.
But he never spoke about it much.

    We noticed the difference, though. It was
the way he looked at people. Now he looks at
them straight, whoever they are. Rabbis,
priests, centurions. None of this looking at the
ground and shuffling out of the way, now. As my
sister said: he looks like a man who's got his
pride back.

## Shepherds visit Jesus

*READ: LUKE 2:15–20*
*A child in Bethlehem speaks*

They all laughed at me when I told them.
They said, 'What was it like?'
And I said, 'What was what like?'
And they said, 'The baby, of course.'
And I said, 'It was small.'
Well, what did they expect it to be like?

*Christmas*
*characters*

### Wise Men visit Herod

*READ: MATTHEW 2:1–6*

*A Scribe speaks*

You would have thought they would know something like that, if they were so wise. These men from the east. But I suppose that is the kind of ignorance one has, if one studies the stars rather than the scriptures.

We would not expect Herod to know, of course. He makes a pretence of studying but it is only so the people will think him a proper Jew. We are not fooled. It pays to play along as far as Herod is concerned.

But these men from the east. These so-called scholars. 'Where is the Messiah to be born?' they asked. One would expect serious scholars to know such a thing. But no. They seemed to have no idea. They were just following a star. And then they left. As if the Messiah might actually have been born. Without us knowing!

### Wise Men visit Jesus

*READ: MATTHEW 2:7–12*

*A woman from Bethlehem speaks*

It still hurts when I think about it. Even now, whenever I hear a horse galloping I feel frightened. They came at dawn: a few on horses and the rest marching, and spreading out through the village. I can hear the shouting now, and the screaming and swearing. Worst of

*Christmas characters*

all was the crying of the children. My young brother Nathan was among the ones the soldiers killed.

It was the king's order, apparently. They were to kill all the children. And they did. That's power for you. Kings! Crush the poor and destroy the opposition.

Someone said he hoped that the child Herod was after had escaped and would come back one day for revenge. Well, if he escaped, good luck to him!

But we don't need revenge. What good would that do? We don't need another king.

Not unless he is a king who lives with the likes of us.

Not unless he knows what it is like to feel so tired he could drop; and to go to bed hungry.

Not unless he is quicker at giving than he is at making demands.

Not unless he can heal people rather than bleed them.

Not unless he has a real way of making peace.

Not unless he is willing to die for his people and not just rule over them.

Not unless he can overcome hatred and death rather than just destroy his personal enemies.

But what kind of king would that be?

*Can you think of carols that would connect these readings and reflections? Do you think the 'characters' should be in costume? If so, what sort of costume?*

*Christmas characters*

# Sightings

*Nativity narratives*

Kathy Galloway

I thought I saw some shepherds yesterday.
They were just going about their business,
or hanging about, as people do,
passing the time, waiting for something to happen,
something to break the dullness of the days.
When something did, it was a bit of a shock.
But they went along anyway.
I thought I saw some shepherds yesterday.

I thought I saw some angels yesterday.
You wouldn't pay them much attention,
unless you were looking in a certain way.
Usually they look quite ordinary,
though they have a way of turning up
just when they're most required –
lending a hand, encouraging you on,
surprising you, and bringing messages
that set you off in quite a new direction.
But yesterday they were all excited,
'Come on, we've got good news for you,
come and see.'
I thought I saw some angels yesterday.

I thought I saw Mary yesterday.
She was sitting by her child's bed,
and he was sleeping.
It was a hospital bed;
she tried six hospitals before one would take him.
Because he was a drug user,
he'd been sleeping rough,
and he'd got gangrene in his leg.
He lost his leg. He was nineteen years old.
There was such pain in her face
but there was such love too,
as she sat there, keeping the night watch
by her homeless child.

I thought I saw Mary yesterday.

I thought I saw Joseph yesterday.
He was pushing a pram,
and there was a baby in it.
It wasn't his baby. It was someone else's child.
No one would have blamed him
if he'd said, 'Okay, that's it. I'm out of here.'
It's a big thing, to take on someone else's child
and love it like your own.
But he loved the baby's mother,
and he knew it would be hard for her alone.
There's a lot of stigma attached
to being a single mum.
And everybody says he's awful good with the baby.
I thought I saw Joseph yesterday.

I thought I saw Jesus yesterday.
He was born at an inconvenient time,
to parents who had to leave their home.
Maybe they were refugees – who knows?
Anyway, their future was uncertain.
But he was lovely, tiny, newborn,
and his parents marvelled, as parents do,
at his little toes and fingers,
and they dreamed dreams for him,
and he gave the future hope for them.
And everyone who looked at him
was somehow changed,
as if they saw life in a different way,
through his newborn, full-of-wonder, eyes.
I thought I saw Jesus yesterday.
But maybe it was just a baby.

*If used as part of worship during Advent, well-known carols (and maybe less familiar ones, such as The Aye Carol from Innkeepers and Light Sleepers) could be used to see whether these words shed new light on the images with which we've become too comfortable and which are anything but incarnational ('but little Lord Jesus no crying he makes').*

*Sightings*

# John

Ruth Burgess

People don't come to you by chance, John.
No one goes into the desert by accident:
you go there when you are driven,
you go there when you must –
when the choices are few.

'Repent.
Turn around.
Change.
You are here knowing that God is angry with you;
you are here empty-handed;
you are here not knowing what will happen next;
your good deeds cannot save you –
I cannot save you either.
This is only water,
water to show that you want to change,
that you want to be clean.
After me comes the one
who knows what you're like –
who will burn up the rubbish with fire.'

Not an easy preacher, John.
Would you have gone to hear him?
Would you have walked into the water?

*The questions with which this ends deserve
reflection. The best setting for this short piece, and
the Gospel passage on which it is based – read
beforehand – is silence. The silence could create
space between the questions, too. The wider
context could include a symbol of 'turning around',
wanting to change: e.g. dropping a stone into a
bowl of water, or burning in a candle flame a paper
on which a reason for 'repentance' has been written.*

MATTHEW 3:1–2

46

# Follow me

*A story for six voices*

## Jan Sutch Pickard

READ MARK 1:16–20

'Follow me,'
he said – and we did.
We let go of the heavy wet nets,
the tough strands of tarred rope:
our strong hands
were empty – we let go
of all we knew how to do,
our livelihood, our identity –
to follow a dream,
a job description
that no one in their senses
would take seriously.
'Follow me,'
he said – and we did.

READ MARK 2:13–17

'Follow me,'
he said – and I did.
Tax collecting never made me popular,
but it put a roof over my head
and bread on my table –
bitter bread, because grabbed and grudged.
He invited me to become
no longer dog in the manger
but host at the feast.
He came right under my roof
sharing my bread
and showing me how to share
with all the rest.
'Follow me,'
he said – and I did.

*MARK 1–10*

*Follow me*

READ MARK 7:25–30

'Go,' he said.
'Let the children be fed first –
why should the dogs eat their bread?'
But I would not be turned away:
hoping for healing,
hungry for justice,
I stood my ground and argued:
'In God's household
even the dogs are fed.'
Seeing my faith,
he told me to go home
and find my daughter healed.
'Go,' he said – and I did.

READ MARK 10:17–22

'Follow me,'
he said, for I had asked him
the next step on a journey
of personal salvation.
He reminded me
of all the good things
I already knew and did.
So nothing was left to do –
I was ready to go.
'Now sell all you have,'
he said. 'Give it away to the poor.'
How could I let go just like that –
lighten the load,
shed my responsibilities,
become someone I did not know?
What would be left?
'Follow me,' he said

but with heavy heart
I shook my head.


*READ MARK 10:46–52*

'Come,'
he said – and I did,
following his voice
through the crowd on the edge of town.
I needed wait no longer:
my voice had been heard
calling for change,
crying out for a fresh start –
even though it meant
casting off old ways,
no longer the needy person everybody knew.
'Come,' he said
and I saw what God could do.
'Your faith has healed you,'
he told me. 'Now go.'
He never said, 'Follow me' –
but, as I could see, there was no other way.


*One person reads the Bible passages, the others*
*take the reflections in turn. Between the readings*
*the congregation could sing verses of 'Will you come*
*and follow me' (the Summons).*

*Follow me*

# Zacchaeus

Norman Shanks

*Luke 19:1–10*

My name is Zacchaeus. I know I've rather a nerve expecting you to listen to me, but I feel there's something I've just got to tell you about. I hope it's all right if I stand up here to talk to you. As you see, I'm not very tall or striking to look at – the sort of person you go past in the street without a second glance. Standing up here helps you to hear me and it's easier too for me to see you. In fact that's somehow how all this started – from trying to get a better view in a crowd.

Perhaps I should explain. I'm a civil servant – or more correctly I used to be a civil servant, until just a few days ago. Not the most popular of professions you might say! Nobody really understands tax-collectors; and yet after all somebody has to do it. They seem to think we are on the side of the Romans – traitors against our own people. We are accused of being cheats, of currying favour with the rich and exploiting the poor – when all along I was only doing my job, as well as I could. It's the system that's unjust, and that's the government's fault – the Roman government, I mean!

But all that is in the past now. My life has been turned upside down. I live in Jericho – some of you may have been there. It's in the Jordan valley, not very far from Jerusalem. I've a wife and three children, and on the whole we have a reasonable life so far as that's possible being a tax-collector (I'm not quite the most popular man about town, as I've said, and that's been hard for the wife and children at times too).

For some months I'd been hearing stories about a man from Nazareth who's been going around Galilee, and some of the other territories too – Jesus bar-Joseph. His father had a very good reputation as a carpenter, an excellent craftsman, a man of integrity. But this Jesus was something else – a kind of travelling rabbi, but with a difference. They were saying all sorts of things about him – that he was drawing crowds wherever he went; that he was healing people who had been ill for years; that he was talking about God and telling stories that made the faith of our mothers and fathers come alive in a new way; that he was ruffling the feathers of the authorities, who were getting really uncomfortable about his popularity and the challenge he was bringing to the old settled ways of believing and behaving. And they said he had a real motley crew of close followers – outsiders and layabouts, fishermen and revolutionaries, housewives and women of ill repute, even the odd tax-collector!

And then I heard he was coming to Jericho, and that made me think. Maybe, just maybe, if I could see Jesus it would help me to sort things out a bit better. I've tried to lead a good life, I've tried to do my job well – even though, as I've said, that often left me feeling lonely, a social outcast almost. I've tried to support my wife and children and look after them as well as I can. But there's always seemed to be something missing – as if I didn't really believe in myself, didn't believe in anything, didn't know what to believe in. It all seemed shallow, empty, meaningless, going nowhere.

And then there was that day. I can't believe it was only last week; so much has happened since then, it feels much longer ago than that. Last week in Jericho the crowds started gathering early. There were people shoulder to shoulder all along the streets, and I wondered how on earth I was going to manage to see him. I know it wasn't the most dignified thing to do – hardly befitting a tax-collector; but I was really desperate. It wasn't just

*Zacchaeus*

*Zacchaeus*

curiosity, something much deeper and more insistent than that – and the sycamore tree was so handy.

And when Jesus came past he stopped under my tree. Some of the people with him tried to hurry him on, as if they knew I was paid by the Romans and he shouldn't be wasting time on the likes of me. But he looked straight at me and talked to me. It was as if he saw right into my heart. He reached out to me, he understood me, he had a word of hope for me; he said he wanted to come and visit our house – to stay with us – and hardly anyone ever wanted to cross our threshold or be seen associating with us.

Since then my life has been turned upside down. And I get the feeling that all sorts of other things have changed, are still changing, won't ever be the same again. I can't say I understand even the smallest part of what's happening. Somehow the things that mattered before are of no consequence – stability, security, having enough money to meet our needs and putting some aside on top of that for a rainy day. My poor wife and family don't understand it all either – but they're caught up in this too of course. He touched their hearts as well in a personal way when he came to our house. There's a new restlessness and urgency about life. But there's also this deep inner peace. He's completely changed the way we look at things: it was something he said about finding life by giving it away, and about the sense of belonging together that he communicated. It's so hard to describe how just being with him makes such a difference. And somehow he stays with you even if he's not there – and you still belong and you see how important it is that other people should know and feel they belong too; there's a kind of openness, a reaching out, a generosity. I got a feeling I've never had before, that I was close to

God and God was close to me, and people like me on the margins, the outsiders, the victims. I think he has a special part he wants us to play ... Oh I wish I could describe it better ...

But what I really want to tell you about is when he entered Jerusalem a few days later. When he left my home he asked me if I wanted to come with him – and I didn't know what to say. It all seemed so risky and I didn't want it to seem as if I was abandoning the family; but my wife encouraged me to go. As we got near Jerusalem he asked two of his friends to go and find a colt, a donkey in fact. It was as if he knew exactly where they'd find it and, as with so much else, I didn't really understand. What on earth was he wanting a donkey for? But he rode on it into Jerusalem and the reception he got was phenomenal. I don't know what people were expecting. I don't think everyone was happy; there was such a commotion that I'm sure the authorities were afraid things were getting out of control. People spread out their coats along the way – the red carpet treatment. There were palm branches waving everywhere – it was like a victory parade. And the noise! Fever pitch. And I'm sure that if Jesus had wanted the crowd to do anything at that point they would have done it.

But there were more surprises in store. The mood changed. It wasn't as if things turned nasty – far from it. Jesus started weeping – he said he was weeping for the city of Jerusalem itself. I don't think anyone understood – utterly baffling. And then everyone dispersed, went away quietly in different directions. Jesus went to spend the night with his friends at Bethany. And then the next day ... but I'll have to save that for another time.

For now I just want to say that I have no idea

*Zacchaeus*

what lies ahead for me or for Jesus. I am so excited and surprised by what has already happened. My heart is singing. My life has been changed for ever. I'm aware of so many wonderful possibilities – not only for me, but somehow for so much more than that. It's as if there is something new, something really big opening up all around. The world is changing, the world will change. It sounds a bit political, I know – and it is. But it's like an invitation to join a treasure hunt! And inside me there's a deep joy that can never be shaken, a trust in God's promise and purposes that nothing will remove, a hope that will survive all disappointments and setbacks. I want other people to have the chance to meet Jesus too. **Amen**

*This meditation was delivered in Iona Abbey on Palm Sunday 1998 at the start of the 'Experiencing Easter' programme, which included interactive Bible studies involving reflection on the events of the Passion narrative through the eyes of some of the participants. In the context, folk may have been expecting a straightforward sermon (it was delivered from a pulpit rather than a sycamore tree). It was a demonstration that this approach works well when least expected.*

Zacchaeus

# I am Mary and I am Martha

### Kate McIlhagga

Lord of earth and sky,
as Martha did
I welcome you into the house of my heart;
as Mary did
I welcome you into the home of my thoughts:
In service,
in listening,
I welcome you.

Like Martha, I'm distracted:
so many calls on my time ...
I run here and there,
starting this and that,
never spending long enough,
giving people the impression
that I'm too busy for them.

Like Mary, I choose:
choose to slow down,
choose to sit at your feet,
choose to offer you
my ministry of listening.
Save me from feeling guilty
about the kitchens of the world:
the hot spots, the action areas
and help me to identify with your compassion
and your presence –
there as everywhere.

Welcomed and welcoming Christ,
may all sisters come together
into your presence
and together eat at your table
the meal you have prepared for us;
that from the kitchen of your suffering
a banquet may be prepared
for all to eat.

*First read the passage; enter into it.*
*Let God's Spirit pray through you.*

*Luke 10:38–42*

# The vine

Jan Sutch Pickard

JOHN 15:1–9

Close your eyes and imagine you are a plant.
Not any plant, a particular kind:
a climbing, clinging plant grown against a wall,
the sunny wall of a house in a hot country;
but it is a country where you are at home,
and you grow well.
You have been planted here
by the owner of the house
because you will grow well
and because you will give welcome shade.
So a trellis has been built –
a framework of weathered wood –
and you have sent out your tendrils onto the trellis,
taken hold and are growing there, too,
your luxuriant leaves shading the terrace underneath,
and the benches where people can sit
in the heat of the day.

You have been here a long time.
Your main stem is old and gnarled,
rough to the touch but beautiful in its own way.
Your roots are deep.
Feel them going down into the earth,
unseen, but still as much part of you
as the leaves that dance in the breeze.
Feel your roots seeking water deep down,
drawing nourishment into your whole being.
Feel your leaves draw energy from the sun
and turn it, in their cells, into strength
for the whole of you.
Feel your tendrils alive,
sensitively seeking new directions
in which you can grow,
and holding on to rough stone and warm wood
so that the wind does not damage you.
Feel your fruits forming, filling out,

becoming juicy, delicious, nourishing.
Feel how each part of you is connected
and draws strength from the other parts.
Feel joy in being the healthy fruitful plant
that God made you to be.

People are coming down the track,
a group of people talking.
They come to the house, stop on the terrace.
Someone from the house brings them cool drinks.
They sit in your shade, talking.
Mostly they are listening to one man,
who seems to be explaining something to them.
They look puzzled.
Suddenly he reaches out, touches your stem,
gestures to your leaves and fruit, and says,
'I am the vine.'

*Use this meditation (possibly with instrumental
music in a couple of pauses in the text) as an
introduction to the Gospel reading.*

*The vine*

# Canaanite mother

Joy Mead

A Canaanite mother came to him angry and alone;
with purpose but no necessity for meaning,
gut feeling being enough.

The child stayed behind:
a torn-apart self
in her dark world, disturbed
by unresolved relationship;
awaiting the coming of spring
and her own flowering.

There was no escaping her,
this unnamed mother
from a despised people.
She made him listen;
gave him vision
and behind her back
he gave a young life
her own balanced centre
of becoming.

*This could be used as part of a Bible study in which members of the group are invited to say what happened in their own words, from the woman's point of view. This third-person version gives another angle on the story. A song which springs to mind is 'The strangest of saints' (Wild Goose Resource Group:* Heaven Shall Not Wait*).*

*Another (possibly complementary) way of accompanying the Gospel passage, followed by the poem, in worship, would be a sequence of slides of children – looking lost, lonely, hungry, angry – and/ or a solo voice singing 'A touching place' (Wild Goose Resource Group:* Love from Below*).*

Mark 7:24–30

58

# We are the sheep

Jan Sutch Pickard

### The Sheep

We are the sheep –
flocking together,
feeling safe together,
following each other ...
Sometimes silly,
sometimes confused,
always hungry:
not meat eaters
but gentle creatures,
keeping our heads down
if we can feed in green pastures ...
sometimes wandering on stony ground,
scattering on dark and cloudy days,
getting lost – grateful to be found ...
With our soft wool
very huggable,
with our soft heads
very muggable ...
simple, sociable, needing a leader
hoping to be looked after ...
We are the sheep.

### Wolf

This is the wolf.
Mothers warn their children about it –
even rottweilers tremble.
It is lean and mean
and greedy.
Sometimes it wears sheep's clothing
and sneaks into the flock.
It is never far away,
and what it likes best
is to creep up and
SNATCH
the sheep!

*John 10:7–18*

### Hired Man

This is the hired man –
not a real shepherd,
he's just doing a job.
They are his living;
who said he should die for them?
He does not own the sheep
or know their names.
They do not know his voice.
Their constant bleating annoys him:
he cannot be expected to meet all their needs.
Sheep are so stupid!
He does not give a toss
he blames his boss.
Why should he care for the flock?
When the wolf walks in
he saves his own skin.


### Thief

This is the thief –
a real villain –
a mugger, a vandal.
All he wants to do
is to steal and spoil and smash things up
and – if he's pushed to it –
he'll kill.
He doesn't use the door:
he comes over the wall.
He is no kind of hero;
he's not just 'wicked'
he's not just 'bad'
he's what we hate and cannot escape.
He's what's gone wrong in our lives:
he's the devil in all of us.

*We are the sheep*

## The Door

This is the door.
Whoever comes in this way
will be safe
their life will be whole.
They will be free to come and go.
They will be fed.
They will be at home with God.

*(This play ends with a prayer)*

## The Shepherd

Jesus – you are our shepherd.
You care for us – and show us
what caring really means.

You know each of us by name.
We are beginning to recognise
your voice speaking to us
in our restless, noisy, anxious lives.

You gave up your life for us.
You did not run away.
No one took it: you gave it.
You show us how to live
in God's way, in God's love.

You are the door to the fold:
to a community
which is not just a place of refuge
but a place where we are loved
and find courage to go out
into the streets.

You care for others
outside the church.
You reach out to them
and call them by name.

*We are the sheep*

Help us to care for others
as we are cared for.
Help us not to be afraid,
or sheepish about our faith,
but to follow you
in God's way, in God's love.

*This was written to be narrated by one or more
voices, while other members of the group mimed
the different characters, ranging through the whole
congregation. It has been used to great effect in all-
age worship. It would also lend itself to a puppet
play. It is important that the prayer is treated
differently from the earlier sections – maybe the
words could be printed out, or projected, so that the
congregation can pray it together.*

We are the sheep

# A child

Ruth Burgess

I hesitated when he called me –
my mum had told me about strangers.
I had watched the men shouting at each other,
wondering what it was
that had made them so angry.
And then he'd come
and sat down on the roadside
and they'd all gone quiet.
He looked at them
sadly, as if they'd hurt him, somehow
and then he raised his face
and his eyes met mine, and he smiled.
He held out his arms
as if he wanted to give me a hug.
He looked kind, but I was afraid.
They were all watching me ...
I wasn't sure what to do.
I looked at him again;
it was as if he needed a cuddle
and he knew I could give him one.
I ran to him and snuggled up to him.
I could feel his pain, he needed me then,
and I could feel his love too.
His arms were safe and strong.
After a minute he turned me round
to face them and he spoke to them –
something about welcome and children –
and they looked at him and looked ashamed.
Then he hugged me again,
talked to me, found out my name,
made me laugh, made me feel loved –
like my mum loves me.
Then he kissed me and told me to go home
and I never saw him again.

*MARK 10:33–37*

# Rock and stumbling block

Jan Sutch Pickard

Matthew 16:13–28

He called me a rock –
and then a stumbling block.
What do I do now?
First there was that question out of the blue –
'Who do people say the Son of Man is?'
An academic kind of question,
not touching us directly.
We told him what we'd heard folk say.
Then he looked me straight in the eye
'And you, who do you say I am?'
And I came straight back –
it's my way – though I'm still not sure
if they were my words:
'You are the Messiah, the son of the living God.'
And he called me a rock.
He called me Peter, the Rock,
and said, 'On this rock I will build my Church.'

And – I confess – I felt proud:
being picked out as the right man for the job,
becoming a Church Leader,
carrying the keys of the Kingdom of Heaven,
speaking words of authority
with such power ...
I'll use it responsibly, of course.

And then he said
'Don't say anything about this to anyone.'
And while I was still taking that in,
he began to talk about it all coming to an end –
before it had really begun.
Such an end, I didn't want to imagine.
I couldn't bear to look ahead, so I looked back
at the good times we'd had, the fellowship,
and at his promise that I'd be
the foundation stone of his Church:

something solid and lasting.
But now he was talking about endings,
about risk and uncertainty,
suffering and shame and death.

I caught his arm and shouted
'Heaven forbid!
This can't happen. I won't let it!'
Then he spun round
and looked me straight in the eye
and called me 'a *stumbling block'*.
So that's the kind of rock I am –
the kind left lying in the road,
a waste of space, in the way.

First off, he said my words came from God;
no human being could have put it the way I did.
I don't know where the words came from –
they just seemed right at the time.
Jesus has more of God about him
than anyone I've ever known –
anyone, I think, in the history of the world.
Not just the things he does – the healings,
the miracles, his teaching,
his challenge to travel on –
but the way he is, the way he looks us in the eye,
and fills us with his life.
'Son of the living God' – I spoke as I found,
though I didn't fully understand what it might mean.
And for that he called me a rock.

The second time round, he said
*'You think as men think, not as God thinks.'*
I had seen all that goodness going to waste.
Hearing his hard words
about dying, about folk destroying him

*Rock and
stumbling block*

before his work was half done –
how could God let that happen? –
of course I protested,
of course I wanted to stop it!
Being a Church Leader didn't prepare me for this.
I thought my words could forbid it,
so I cried out against it.
And he called me a stumbling block.

How can one person be both a rock
and a stumbling block?
Can it be me?
Standing in the road, as though turned to stone;
overwhelmed by words I don't understand
and lost for any I can say from my heart;
not knowing whether to look forward or back.
If you build a Church on me, it won't budge either.

How can I shake off this stony state I'm in?
How can I begin to follow the friend
on whose moving Word I need to build?
How do I take up my cross?

*This monologue could be used as a way into Bible
study. It has been used in a reflective evening
service with the Gospel passage read first, then a
silence, then the monologue, then more silence,
then prayers of confession.*

*It could also be linked with the other 'Peter'
meditation,* I'd had enough *(p. 79).*

## Rock and stumbling block

# Four people who met Jesus

John Bell

One of the purposes of preaching is to flesh out the text of the Bible, enabling the ancient words to impinge on contemporary experience.

These four monologues seek to do the same, by articulating, in contemporary – and even vernacular – language, the experience of four people whom Jesus met.

Each of the monologues is the result of group reflection by people who were willing to enable the biblical characters to be real in the present tense, rather than locked in a Victorian stained-glass time warp.

Each of these, with the Gospel passage on which it is based, could form part of the Ministry of the Word in one service. Or a youth service, for instance, could be constructed around the four of them.

Wild Goose songs which relate to the issues raised here are: 'We cannot measure how you heal', 'The beggar' (both from Love From Below); 'Lord of life, we come to you', 'Lord Jesus Christ, lover of all' (both from There Is One Among Us).

# The leper

John Bell

You should have seen the priest's face
when I arrived at his door.

I suppose me grinning all over didn't help.

He knew my family ... especially my father
who had helped to build the parish hall.
He and the priest were very close,
but they never talked about me.

You see, when you get leprosy,
you don't belong any more ...
you don't belong to your family
and you don't belong to the Church.

This was the priest
who had confirmed the diagnosis,
the priest who had sent me from the sanctuary
never to return,
asking God to have mercy on my soul ...
the kind of thing you'd say to a criminal
en route to the gallows.

And here I was back ... seven years later,
minus an arm,
presenting myself as cured.

He didn't know what to say.
He didn't know which book to look for
or which page to turn.

He had only been taught how to
send lepers away ceremoniously.
He had never learned how to receive them back.

It took a long while ... not just finding the book ...

*Matthew 8:1–4*

it took a long while for him to come within a foot,
within three feet, of me.

He wanted me to tie a blindfold on myself ...
till I said, 'I've only got one arm ...
you'll have to do it.'

But he couldn't bring himself to touch me.
So he asked me to put a cloth sack over my head,
and then he took a pin and began to stick it
into parts of my body,
saying, 'Where am I touching?'
And every time I knew.
Every time it hurt.
The sensation was back.

He even pushed the pin into my stump and I yelled.
Actually I yelled louder than I needed to,
but I reckoned that
if this guy was going to give me a hard time,
he should feel some of the pain too.

Then he took the bag off my head
and said, 'How is this possible?'

I said,
'It's possible because in a world
where everybody, including the Church,
has kept back and avoided me,
somebody ...
one man ...
touched me;
no he didn't just touch me,
he embraced me as if I were the brother
he'd always wanted to find.'

The leper

The priest didn't ask his name.
It was as if he knew
and as if he were disappointed
that what religion turned away from,
God embraced.

The leper

# The woman caught in adultery

John Bell

I wasn't ill.

Oh there were rumours.
I knew about them before,
and I heard about them afterwards.

I was supposed to have given
half the men in the village syphilis.
I was rumoured to be the cause
of two women giving birth to deaf children.

The phrase people would use was:
'He must have been with Annie.'

If an apprentice arrived late
and bleary-eyed for work
on a Monday morning,
somebody would say,
'Were you with Annie last night, then?'

If somebody started scratching ...
their head or their groin ...
someone else would suggest,
'Looks as if you've been with Annie.'

But none of them had ever 'been' with me.

My reputation developed
because I had twins outside wedlock.
I gave my virginity to a man
who said he'd marry me.
Two days later, he got drowned at sea.
And because he came from a decent family
and also because I loved him,
I never said he was the father
of the children in my womb.

*JOHN 8:1–11*

I suppose if there had been just one child,
it would have been easier.
But when there were two,
the gossips had a field day ...
saying that Samuel, the oldest,
looked very like John Jacobson the timber merchant
and Matthew, the youngest, looked more like
James Mitchell the undertaker.

I had put up with this for ten years,
and I had never retaliated,
and I had never given myself to any other man ...

until ... and I don't know why ...
I allowed myself to be swept off my feet
by a married man
who said that his wife couldn't understand him.

I gave him my sympathy,
I gave him my time.
I never thought it would go further than friendship.
I had no idea that his wife
was watching every move.

She chose her time well,
and she brought eight, nine, ten men with her
who wanted to have their fantasies confirmed.

They called me a whore, a filthy bitch ...
and much, much more.
They dragged me by the hair through the streets,
into the public square.
Old men prodded me with their sticks.
Young men tramped on my fingers.
Women spat.

*The woman
caught in adultery*

At six o'clock, they were going to stone me.
At ten to six, he knelt down beside me ... and,
whatever he said,
they disappeared,
and when he said, 'I forgive you,'
I knew that I was healed,
even though I had never been sick.

The woman
caught in adultery

# The cripple at the pool

John Bell

*John 5:1–13*

The thing to know about me
is that I had no conception who he was.

I contracted polio when I was about six
and there was nothing that could be done.

So, when I was twelve,
my father took me to the pool.
Other boys got a bar mitzvah,
I got taken to a shrine ...
well, not really a shrine ...
there was this thing about the water moving
and first in afterwards got cured.

Listen, I've lain there for 38 years
and there were no cures,
just a lot of fantasising.

I suppose you might say
I had got comfortable there.
I mean, I might have been a cripple,
but I could smile and talk.
I said hello to everybody by name
and it paid dividends ...
people put money in my hat.
It wasn't the best existence,
but there was worse.

And then up comes this total stranger
Now when I say total, I mean total.
I never knew him, he never knew me.

He didn't ask who I was or tell me his name.

He just said,
'Do you want to get better?'

I felt like saying,
'Do you think I've been lying here on this stretcher
for forty years
just to get a sun tan?'

But I didn't.
I didn't like his question.
It threatened me.
To get better would mean becoming responsible.
To get better would mean walking and working
and putting pennies in other people's hats.

You know, I nearly said, 'Leave me alone.'

But there was something in his directness,
something in the way he cut across
forty years of apathy ...
so I said yes.
And ever since then,
I've been standing on my own feet ...
in more ways than one.

But I didn't know him.
And when the intelligentsia began to ask questions
about who had cured me,
I couldn't give them a name.

All I could say was,
'The man who asks disturbing questions.'

*The cripple at
the pool*

# The haemorrhaging woman

John Bell

*Luke 8:40–48*

Now don't you get me wrong –
for everybody else does.
I am not a wee quiet mouse
and I never have been.

I mean, with a name like 'Big Isa'
I could hardly ever have been 'petite'.

I was always in the limelight.
I always chased the boys – they never chased me,
and if ever there was a go-as-you-please,
I'd be there singing 'Ten Guitars'
or 'Crystal Chandeliers'
or 'Hands, Knees and Boomps a Daisy'
... with actions.

I used to be 23 stone ...
many of which weren't stones at all,
but sherbet bon bons, clotted cream caramels
and chocolate eclairs.

I was 36 when the bleeding started,
but, of course, it was never called 'bleeding',
it was a 'discharge' according to the doctor
... just another aspect of 'women's troubles'.

I says, 'Listen doctor, the only trouble
that we women have
is men like you.
I'm not discharging ...
what do you think I am – a sewage pipe?
And I don't have "women's troubles" ...
I'm losing something like a pint of blood a week.'

Well, the doctor said there was nothing for it.

So I tried other options:
copper bangles
a rabbit's paw under my pillow
bathing in salt water when there was a full moon.

I went on a seven-day silent retreat.
I paid three weeks' wages to a wee Italian
for crystals which had healed half the folk in Rome.

And all the time, I was losing weight
and losing hope.

'Big Isa' became 'Isa' and then 'Wee Isa'.

And then I heard
that he was coming into our village.
It was my last chance and I knew it.
I thought I might just squeeze through the crowd,
but that was useless,
they were tight packed like sardines.

So ... where I got the strength from I don't know,
but I just got wellied in.
I shoved, I pulled,
I kicked an old man in the shins,
I bit somebody in the arm
who tried to keep me back.
And then ...
then I saw him ...
and I said, 'God, this time – please.'
And I threw myself forward
and just managed to touch his sleeve
before some man who smelt of fish
gave me such a shove
that I fell on my backside.

*The
haemorrhaging
woman*

But that was enough.
It worked ...
though I was a quivering wreck when I realised
that the whole procession had stopped
and everybody was staring in my direction.

He said it was my faith that did it ...
but I had had faith in the doctor before ...
and in the crystals.

It wasn't just my faith. It was him.

The
haemorrhaging
woman

# I'd had enough

Ruth Burgess

I'd had enough.
The last few days had been too full of questions,
too full of surprises that shocked and hurt
and made me wonder.
Was Jesus really alive?
Had our hopes conjured up a ghost in dark rooms
and early morning shadows?
What should I do now?
I did the safe thing – the familiar thing –
the childhood thing –
I went fishing.
The others must have felt like me.
They needed no asking.
They joined me in the boat
and we cast off in the moonlight.
All night we fished,
but there was nothing swimming into our nets –
that was familiar all right, but reassuring,
nothing had really changed.
Perhaps we could pick up the old life again,
abandon the last three wandering years
and do again the old things
that we did well together.
We would not forget him – we couldn't.
His stories, his encounters,
the way he changed people he met,
the way he looked at us and loved us –
those memories would always stay with us,
stirring up warm recollections inside us.
We could live with those thoughts.
But now we were ordinary people again,
part of the crowd – earning our living,
enjoying home comforts
and family laughter and tears.

*JOHN 21:1–14*

As light dawned we sailed homewards.
A man shouted to us from the shore,
to put out our nets –
he must have been able to see the fish
swarming near the boat.
When we did, our net filled,
making it too heavy to haul aboard.
I was about to shout my thanks
when John pulled my arm
and said, 'That man, it's Jesus.'
My world turned round –
new light flooding into its darkness –
I jumped from the boat and waded towards him.
My friends followed, adjusting the boat's sails
to compensate for the net's weight.

*Do you think the Gospel reading should come before or after or be replaced by this meditation? With a small group, would a picture of the encounter described by John be a good focus, or maybe a simple image – of a fish, for example, or a photograph or slides of light dancing on water?*

He must have been fishing too –
on a beach fire I could smell his catch grilling,
and he said to me, 'Bring some more fish
to put on the fire.'
I turned back and helped drag in the net –
a mass of slithering scales dancing in the dawn light –
and then he spoke again, 'Come and have breakfast.'
What kind of a ghost was this –
that cooked our breakfast?
He handed us bread and hot fish
and sat down with us to eat.
A thousand questions were on my lips,
as I shared that meal – and I wanted to ask them.
There, in that mixture of bread and fish and friends,
I knew that I still loved him,
that I could not keep him in my memories.
He is part of who I am –
what I have to do and be –
and I want to be with him.

*I'd had enough*

# Pilgrimage is a circular route

Kate McIllhagga

Rome to Canterbury
Derry to Iona
Iona to Bamburgh
Bamburgh to Bradwell
Whitby to Whithorn —
pilgrimage is a circular route,
following the scuffmarks of history.

Beware the onslaught of nostalgia,
look out for sickly sentimentality:
the saintly monk who never broke a fingernail
or into sweat.
Remember, rather, and walk
in the footsteps of countless refugees,
tramping the forests of fear,
camping out in the fields of hopelessness;
the scent, not of crushed myrtle but panic,
the sound, not of the lark, but of the sniper's bullet,
soaring, seeking warm flesh.

Seek then to remember
the brave steps of Mandela,
the unfinished work of Luther King,
the courage and compassion of Romero.
Carry with you also Herstory:
Margaret of Scotland and Hilda of Whitby;
Clothilde and Bertha, persuasive princesses;
Elizabeth Fry and Emily Pankhurst,
who broke open prisons and set free prisoners.

Remember all the invisible ones,
walk in the footmarks of the forgotten ones.

And when your place of departure
becomes also your place of arrival

*HEBREWS 11:8–10, 18–16*

and you 'know the place for the first time':*
What has changed? What have you indulged?
In seeking what have you found?
In penance have you travelled
the long hard road to restitution?
And as you step off and out of the procession,
what of you will those who continue
carry until you meet again?
What of them do you bring to us?


*(T.S. Eliot).


*This reflection could be accompanied by slides –
not too many – but to pick up the names and
images of places and people, so that we use our
imagination and our eyes.*

    *It is a way of bringing the powerful words, and
remembering, of Hebrews 11 closer to home. How
would you bring them closer still? Members of the
congregation could be invited to thank God for folk
who have been part of their own faith journey, and
similarly for places.*

## Pilgrimage is a
## circular route

# Doing Bible role play

# Doing Bible role play

Anna Briggs

The minimum time that should be allowed is one and a half hours; an ideal time would be two to two and a half hours. You need a group of 12–36 people and a leader. The instructions that follow are for the benefit of the leader.

* Choose a short passage from the Gospels, selected to relate to the theme of your time together.

* Read the story, identify the characters, e.g. 'Jesus', 'Disciples', 'Crowd', 'Boy with loaves and fishes'.

* Divide group into small groups, one for each character, as identified. People can be put into groups by choice or by random selection. Move people and chairs to sit in these groups.

* Ask people to listen as you read the story again, imagining themselves into the character, hearing the story from this point of view.

* In the groups discuss the feelings and reactions experienced as the character. (10 minutes)

* After ten minutes, ask groups to identify two statements, or two questions, or one question and one statement to be made to other 'characters'. A spokesperson should also be chosen, and it will help if consensus is arrived at. (5 to 10 minutes)

* After five to ten minutes, ask groups to turn to face each other. In turn, each 'character' group is invited to make its statements or ask its questions. Stress before they start that at this time there is to be no verbal response. Someone in each group should note down questions and statements directed at them. (5 to 10 minutes)

* Repeat the process, with groups discussing their collective response to the statements/questions. In the unlikely event that a group gets no question, they may discuss a statement/question to another group and how it reflects on their 'character'. (20 minutes)

* Repeat process of making responses – again, no quick replies. (5 to 10 minutes)

* By this time some salient remarks will have emerged (some by people breaking the 'rules') and the role play can be drawn to a close with some observations about insights revealed.

* Now it's time for a debriefing, with groups briefly telling each other how they felt in the role play, whether the dynamics of the group allowed for their view to be represented, how it felt living inside biblical characters, etc. (10 minutes) In the large group, there can be a long or short discussion on the insights gained in the whole process, and you can be sure the discussion will go on and on after the session is ended.

*Doing Bible role play*

# Epilogue

# Epilogue

### Anna Briggs

Each of us lives in a story of the world – of what it means, how it fits together, what our place in it might be.

Look at a secure toddler, growing to understand herself as the centre of attention, then having to relearn as parents insist she go to sleep when put into the cot. Gradually, at times in confusion, the toddler finds that others sometimes have to come first.

Look at a disturbed child, abused or neglected, then removed from his birth family by unknown authorities. He has learned that no adult can be trusted to keep him safe, so he himself has no inclination to consider the safety or wellbeing of others.

Sometimes the security, the comfort, of our own story is rudely interrupted. There is illness, accident, violence and death. Relationships break and we are forced to rewrite our story whether we like it or not. Of such stuff are major novels, major dramas, made. Novelists and playwrights hold up a mirror to the real world, a mirror which shows us what is possible before it happens to us.

The Bible is just such a story or collection of stories. What eventually became the Bible began as a huge collection of stories, expressed in prose and poetry of many kinds. Those from whom they came wanted to pass on some understandings: about the world, the whole of creation, how it fits together, and what our part in it is. They were creatures of their time, and yet more.

In a huge variety of circumstances and experiences, from birth to death, in war and peace, power and oppression, starvation and plenty, human beings came to understand themselves in relation to an unseen God. No event, no action, is without

consequence, and repeated encounters with justice and mercy track the growth of conscience and freedom from fatalism.

The story of Jesus Christ brings this progression sharply into focus. One human being, someone who can be seen and heard, someone who shares meals, touches and feels, and notices what is going on around him, becomes the one person whose life and death are so singular, so significant, that his story has grasped imaginations around the world for two thousand years, and invoked loyalty and a worldwide movement. Somehow the unseen God is seen, heard, touched and makes us partners and friends.

And he tells stories so that those who hear will understand. The stories are not about planets and stars, but about harvests, flowers, birds, robbers and rescuers, priests and outcasts. The stories are so striking, and ring so true, that we have inherited them in spoken, then in written, form.

These stories, the tales of the people of God, and of one who was understood to be the Son of God himself, were passed on, and written down, not to be gawped at as an ancient curiosity, but to live always for the present day.

So, read the stories not as ancient folklore, the fairy tales of faith, but as you would read your daily paper or watch the TV news.

Find yourself in the story; find the unlikely person, the outcast, the one not mentioned. Ask the questions the text doesn't answer. Where are the wives and children in the house of Simon the Pharisee? How did the woman with the twelve-year period find the strength even to leave her house? Listen to Jesus' answers. Don't take the comfortable option – wriggle with the meaning of them for you.

Write, reflect on the stories. And when you have

*Epilogue*

reflected on your own, do it with other people.

There are so many ways of living through the Gospel stories together.

Use movement, pictures and music to explore the stories. From a pile of newspapers and magazines make a collage exploring the story. Draw, mould clay, act, sing. You can!

Bible role play, as explained by Hans Ruedi Weber and Walter Wink, is a controlled way of living inside a character or group of people in company with others, of asking questions of the other characters, the questions that come from deep inside you, questions that you don't even know are there until you start. (A detailed description of such a method can be found on pages 83–84)

From these approaches come questions that we didn't expect. 'Take my donkey (car/van)? You must be kidding! How am I going to get my goods to market? Do you want my family to starve?' or 'Give everything I own to the poor? But what about my mortgage? I've four children to support – and I've worked hard to get where I am!'

Where do these questions lead you and the members of your group? Can you live in these stories, and grow inside them? Will they help you to be free of the unnamed terrors and burdens of your lives?

When you move away from the text, does the story go with you? Does it surround you and bring you new insight in all your dealings, with friend and stranger?

The writers here have imagined their way into the stories of the Bible, and have moved them on for you, opened them up for you. Can you in turn open them up for other people? Can you tell the stories in their language? Can you live the stories so that they

*Epilogue*

91

see them in action? Can you show them that these stories are a good place to live in?

Sydney Carter wrote: 'Your holy hearsay is not evidence. Give me the Good News in the present tense.' You and I are living in the story now. You and I are telling it.

*Epilogue*

# Songs

A list of the songs suggested throughout this book for use with particular meditations.

**The Aye Carol** from *Innkeepers and Light Sleepers*

**The Beggar** from *Love From Below*

**God It Was Who Said to Abraham** from *Love From Below*

**Lord Jesus Christ, Lover of All** from *There Is One Among Us*

**Lord of Life, We Come to You** from *There Is One Among Us*

**Stand O Stand Firm** from *Many and Great*

**The Strangest of Saints** from *Heaven Shall Not Wait*

**A Touching Place** (Christ's is the world in which we move) from *Love From Below*

**We Cannot Measure How You Heal** from *Love From Below*

**Will You Come and Follow Me** from *Heaven Shall Not Wait*

*All the above songbooks are published by Wild Goose Publications*

# The Iona Community

The Iona Community is an ecumenical Christian community, founded in 1938 by the late Lord MacLeod of Fuinary (the Revd George MacLeod DD) and committed to seeking new ways of living the Gospel in today's world. Gathered around the rebuilding of the ancient monastic buildings of Iona Abbey, but with its original inspiration in the poorest areas of Glasgow during the Depression, the Community has sought ever since the 'rebuilding of the common life', bringing together work and worship, prayer and politics, the sacred and the secular in ways that reflect its strongly incarnational theology.

The Community today is a movement of over 200 Members, around 1,500 Associate Members and about 700 Friends. The Members — women and men from many backgrounds and denominations, most in Britain, but some overseas — are committed to a rule of daily prayer and Bible reading, sharing and accounting for their use of time and money, regular meeting and action for justice and peace.

The Iona Community maintains three centres on Iona and Mull: Iona Abbey and the MacLeod Centre on Iona, and Camas Adventure Camp on the Ross of Mull. Its base is in Community House, Glasgow, where it also supports work with young people, the Wild Goose Resource and Worship Groups, a bimonthly magazine (*Coracle*) and a publishing house (Wild Goose Publications).

For further information on the Iona Community please contact:

The Iona Community

Pearce Institute,

840 Govan Road

Glasgow G51 3UU

T. 0141 445 4561; F. 0141 445 4295

*e-mail:* ionacomm@gla.iona.org.uk